Irish Hares and Seahorses

Edited by Mary Farrell

Norꜩh Coasꜩ Wriꜩers

Content Art created by Mae Gardiner & Sinead Coxhill

ISBN: 978-1-914130-61-8

OTHER TITLES BY IMPSPIRED

It's Like Walking a Tightrope –
by Mary Farrell

Final Flight as the Fog Becomes Night -
By Tim Heerdink

Tir Na NOg –
By Justin Wiggins

Poems of Life –
By William Fearby

The Spiritist –
By Theresa Gaynord

A Body, A Soul –
By Shannon Hopkins

The Girl in the Stone –
By Don Beukes

'*From All of Us to All of You*'

~ Walt Disney 1958 ~

Contents

James Simpson

Sue Steging

Rhona Stephens

Mary Farrell (Editor, Group Leader)

Acknowledgements and Thanks

Our first 'thank you' goes to the 2019 Committee of Causeway u3a (University of the Third Age) who encouraged and supported the setting up of both the North Coast Writers groups. Secondly, we are very grateful to the 2022 Committee for continuing this nurturing relationship as we showcase our work and our first anthology.

With great foresight Causeway u3a embraced alternative technologies in the Spring of 2020 to enable groups such as ours to continue to meet via Zoom. A special 'thank you' goes to Brendan Mullan, whose expertise and infinite patience introduced us all to the wonders of Zoom, opening up our lives each and every week.

We owe a huge debt of gratitude to the School of Arts and Humanities at Ulster University, particularly to Dr Kathleen McCracken, Lecturer in English and Creative Writing, and Dr Frank Sewell, Senior Lecturer in Creative Writing and Irish Literature in English, for all their guidance and encouragement in our writing pursuits.

The writing world, particularly in Northern Ireland, has inclusiveness at its heart. Interacting with other groups, writers and facilitators we have enjoyed a willingness to share experience and learning. We have benefitted greatly from a close association with Portrush Writers Group, This Writing Thing, Burnavon Writers and Foyle u3a Creative Writing Group.

Thanks are extended to the Royal Court Hotel for hosting the launch of our first annual anthology. We could not write a better backdrop for the launch of our combined musings than the dramatic North Coast.

Many writers write mainly for their own amusement and satisfaction while others are brave enough to showcase their work, connecting with other people. Critical in this sharing is the role of an Editor, and so we send our gratitude to Steve Cawte at Impspired Press for his professionalism.

Saving the warmest and biggest thank you for last, we want to thank our ever-patient families and friends for their continued encouragement and assistance. On the surface writing appears to be a solitary pursuit. Nothing could be further from the truth. If it takes a village to raise a child it takes family and friends to foster a writer.

We thank you all.

Acknowledgements of First Publication

Psithurism by Robin Holmes was published in the *Bangor Literary Journal Issue 14*, Spring 2021.

Two Lapwings by Robin Holmes was published in Poetry in Motion, Community Arts Partnership Anthology, *Vision*, 2020.

A Telling Tear by Geraldine Fleming was published in *Impspired magazine*, 1st June 2021.

Menopausal Mermaids - January by Sinead Coxhill was published in Poetry in Motion, Community Arts Partnership Anthology, *Heartland*, 2021.

A Coat of Many Colours by Mae Gardiner was performed on YouTube, August 2020, available on YouTube, https://youtu.be/7iUFzNgImRs

No Walk No Escape by Brenda McAteer was performed at the Orchard Flash Fiction Fair, Armagh, September 2021, available on YouTube, https://youtu.be/fKDjjyA0WUA

Changing Focus and Twilight by Orla McFaul were performed at the Seamus Heaney Homeplace, Bellaghy, December 5th, 2021.

Mercy Killing by Jimmy Milliken was published in Poetry in Motion, Community Arts Partnership Anthology, *Resonance*, 2018.

Damals in Odessa by Jimmy Milliken was performed on Poetry in Motion, National Poetry Day Live Zoom, 27th Sept. 2020, available on YouTube.

Voodoo Child (Slight Return) by Jimmy Milliken was performed at the Seamus Heaney Homeplace, Bellaghy, 5th December 2021.

No Sure Acre by James Simpson was published in *On the Grass When I Arrive: An Anthology of New Writing from Northern Ireland on Place, Home and Belonging.* Edited by B Litvack, 2016.

Lines in the Garden and *Reading a River* by Sue Steging were published in Poetry in Motion, Community Arts Partnership Anthology, *Vision*, 2020.

The Goldfinch by Sue Steging was published in Poetry in Motion, Community Arts Partnership Anthology, *Heartland*, 2021.

All Hallows Eve is in the Collection 'It's like Walking a Tightrope' by Mary Farrell, published September 2021 by Impspired Press.

13 Down, And the Joke's on..., Winter Tree, Up That Hill are in the Collection ' Out of the Chrysalis' by Mary Farrell, published July 2022 by Impspired Press.

Books published since the North Coast Writers Group began, 2019

'Smokes and Birds', James Simpson, Dingle Publishing, 2021.

'It's like walking a Tightrope', Mary Farrell, Impspired Press, 2021

Introduction
By Mary Farrell

North Coast Writers met for the first time on Wednesday, 9th January 2019, in Agherton Church Hall in Portstewart, a small coastal town in Northern Ireland. The number of writers involved proved to be so talented, prolific and enthusiastic that a second Group was formed in September of that year. Meeting weekly since then, initially face-to-face and more recently on Zoom, both Groups have been going from strength to strength.

Irish Hares and Seahorses is their first Annual Anthology.

The Merriam- Webster dictionary states that the word 'Anthology' comes from the Greek word anthología meaning a "gathering of flowers". There are beautiful blooms to be found in this volume, powerful prose rooted in the earth, characters some sweet-smelling some thorny, sinuous shapes of concrete poetry, stanzas of verse which twine and curl like ivy. Tended and pruned collectively by the Group members, seeds from fertile minds were woven into garlands of varied size, length and format.

Distinctive as the Irish Hares of the title, each of the contributors offers a selection in their own unique voice. Birthed in Irish soil, like Seahorses, these voices have also been nourished and invigorated by the fresh winds and flow of the Atlantic tides.

North Coast Writers are delighted to present to you this 'bouquet' enriched by the friendship, encouragement and support we have all shared over the last three years.

Robin Holmes

To everything there is a season

Robin Holmes believes that growing up on a small hill farm in the Mournes Mountains in Northern Ireland was a nurturing and formative experience for his later writing. After attending the University of Ulster, where he studied English Literature and Philosophy, he embarked on a career in social work. His first published poem was in the 1994 'Poetry Now' anthology. Following retirement, Bernie Mc Gill's Creative Writing Class at Flowerfield Arts Centre was a stimulus to a more sustained period of writing.

In 2018 he was Commended in the Bangor Literary Journal's Sixth Annual Poetry Competition and in 2019 he was shortlisted in the same competition. In 2020 his poem 'As if' came fourth after a public online vote for the Eighth Competition. In 2021 he was shortlisted for the BLJ's Forty Words Competition. Robin has also had his work published in the Community Arts Partnership, Poetry in Motion anthology for the last five consecutive years, commencing in 2018. He has given readings of his work at showcase events in Flowerfield Arts Centre and the Seamus Heaney Homeplace.

In January 2019 he was a co-founder with Mary Farrell, of the North Coast Writer's Group. In 2021 he made outdoor location videos for two of his poems 'Psithurism' and 'Fred Dibnah', which are now available on the Bangor Literary Journal's YouTube channel. An audio recording of his short story 'The Iron Horse' is held as part of the permanent exhibition for the Sam Henry Collection by Causeway Coast and Glens Borough Council in Northern Ireland.

Psithurism

For I have bathed in
the tides of forests,
as you may, each morning
in the chilled winter sea.
Not for me an electrocution
of the senses, a saline sledgehammer,
but a still undressing of the mind,
an exchange of clothes, a
putting on of the silken robes
of wildness, an imbibing
of the scent of pine, larch
and spruce, wild garlic;
the fermenting freshness
of all flora, each breath a
a purge into purity.

and whether with birdsong,
in spring's surging symphony,
or the strangulated lament of
a solitary winter straggler,
such accompaniment
delights always; audible
above the trampling underfoot
of twigs, squelch of leaf mould,
my steps in a bossa nova beat
with each breaking breath,
and always, always, the
regiments of upright trunks,
branches, leaves, swaying,
striving, straining towards
a celestial ceiling; recruiting
me to enlist with their
            soft,

        seamless

        psithurism.

TWO LAPWINGS

Seeking a corner   of real estate
    to build an   alluvial apartment,
      a brittle bothy,   to brood and breed.
    Their sartorial crests are ancient antennae,
    attuned to another world, the ebb
      of moon and tide.

    Finally the sky,
   drilled and gouged by
  the curvature of their wings,
   collapses in on itself
    in smithereens
     of awe.

Intoxicated by   Spring's seismic surge,
  they launch into   mid-air, sky skipping,
   a delirious display   of aerial abandonment,
    barnstorming bravado, claws latching,
    a flamboyant flamenco
     of flight.

    Finally the sky,
   drilled and gouged by
  the curvature of their wings,
   collapses in on itself
    in smithereens
     of awe.

A Vigil

Upstairs, in your nursing home ,
the hours laden,
a saturated silence,
my hand through cold steel cot sides
holds yours, an umbilical cord of love.
Our roles reversed now, hands that once
nursed, rocked and fed me.
You are walking through the valley,
the valley of long shadows.
The warmth of your hand oscillates,
a tentative tachograph of life.
When you squeeze my hand,
it is a Morse Code, saying
"I am still here".

Outside, at dusk each evening, the rooks
migrating home, travelling
as if on long pencilled parallel lines,
some in flocks, others are lonesome stragglers,
stricken bombers limping home;
their black wings rise and fall like oars,
gulping the air of the gloaming.
In the distance, a rookery
where leafless branches strangle the setting sun.
A vast, raucous, cawing cacophony
evanesces into an eternal evensong.

One evening, you too became restless,
battling for air, morphine swirling through you
until your breathing dropped to a whisper
and then, you flew away.

Treble Clef
~ Three Haikus~

Beethoven

Your Third, Fifth and Ninth,
tortured symphonic genius,
deafness hearing joy.

Chopin

Consumed consumptive,
heart bleeding into nocturnes,
keys played by snowflakes.

Debussy

Listened to moonlight,
shimmering arpeggios,
unrequited love.

SLIEVE DONARD AND THE CLOUDS

Each day Slieve Donard,
buxom of granite,
wearing her clouds; a model
on a bouldered catwalk.
From the Spring Collection,
Cumulus, puffed and floating
as tufts of bog cotton.
Summer, and Cirrus dangles,
a light, wispy neck scarf.
Autumnal days find her wearing
an inert greatcoat of mist.
Winter moon clouds
lie over her shoulders,
like a mink coat.

and always the light,
framed and fractured,
forceful and fragile,
fantailed sunlight
funnelling into vast
radiating spokes,
puncturing and prising.
Great searchlights
sweeping across
Zeppelin clouds,
raking the sky,
God's fingers,
Relativity speaking.

Geraldine Fleming

"An Owl is mostly air"
Ursula K Le Guin

Geraldine Fleming retired early from an all-consuming career due to ill health. Bereft of purpose in life she found herself drawn into a past interest in creative writing. She is a member of the North Coast Writers Group in Northern Ireland and enjoys writing both prose and poetry.

In 2019, she was Highly Commended in the *Bangor Literary Journal Poetry Competition* Two poems are scheduled for publication in *Community Arts Partnership Anthology, Threshold,* 2022. *Cartographer,* was long listed for the Seamus Heaney Award 2022.

Geraldine has published in a number of journals including *Pendemic, The Crow of Minerva, Neuro Logical Literary Magazine, Selcouth Station, Sledgehammer, Impspired, A New Ulster, Visual Verse, Second Chance Lit* and *Mercurius Magazine.*

Cashel Man

I dreamt the death of a bronze age man
                        a parallax between worlds and aeons

            rivalries seethe and convulse in the otherworld
testing weaknesses in earthbound frontiers
            waiting for that special alignment
            a rupture   scythes open at Samhain
            a fleeting merger   from her realm to his

                    intoxicated by her guising and music
        stretching   open the portal's edge
                        he steps through liminal veils

                                    they dance
                                    embrace
                                    a final kiss

                        then

        exile back to his insoluble world
cast
foetal-curled to his bog hole grave lying south to north
clutching his knees in sacrifice
        image distinct in light and shadow
flex contours from a time when the wind was a howling
grey wolf

Dana's
belly swells
enriching power
her domain assured
she waits in bliss for
the birthing
gods cower
heads hung
unhinged by the hybrid
her daughter still
reigning over
day and night
while
her banished lover's leathered bones are turned over
de-souled in his earthly pit

mists reach out to me beyond logic
a web of spells cleaving to the edge of reality

#Neurasthenia

Tyler had pulled an all-nighter, again. In fact, he had been playing continuously for over forty-three hours. He thought there should be some sense of triumph as he was the last man standing. He had invested hundreds of hours and lost many friends working steadily up the rankings, to this point. One point eight million viewers watched him dispatch his friend Stig in the final level to win the competition. Before he sat down to play he had savoured the thrum of endorphins flooding his veins and arteries. He felt invincible. Now, winning had never felt so hollow. There was no urge to fist pump the air or utter gloating consolations. He didn't even want to watch the congratulations roll on screen or take note of his cash pot. Anti-climax had hit him this time in an instant. The pixelated cover was snatched off his pit of anguish again and the longing to be back online screamed his name.

The detritus of his stint fringed his elite gaming chair. Water bottles emptied and refilled with his darkening urine lined one side of his position. On the other Red Bull cans lay crushed, discarded like the bodies left behind in the game. A haphazard corner cliff of moving crates entombed his long-forgotten family photos and life's essentials. Instinctively he eased the headset off. The heat in the room was stifling, humidity-loaded, a combination of his sweat and the struggling coolers on the PC. The curtains were closed, he had no clue if it was day or night.

He thought it didn't really matter, he hadn't been outside in, well, he didn't really remember the last time. His brain refused to do the calculation. A memory of rain, an impromptu shower releasing the hope of a new-born spring pushed for attention, he found it a painful thought to follow. Too painful. His brain felt a cascade of cauterising explosions, as if it had subsumed the hundreds of devices triggered during the tournament and was releasing them in a rattle of retribution. Tilting back into the headrest he rocked his head from side to side. He pressed his hands over his ears to try to block the sound. Reflex snapped his palms away. The rising heat almost seared his hands. He just couldn't avoid the high frequency buzzing in his ears, it seemed to oscillate, lapping around his brain. As the sound intensified the temperature rose, allied for no logical reason. He imagined he felt his fillings rattling like an aftershock from some unknown event. His heart fibrillation amplified around his body, racing a micro current at laser speed. Flashing after-images filled his entire field of vision even as he closed his eyes. He tried to move his legs, there was no response. He tried his arms, they had moved just a moment ago, no response.

Bile rose from his belly and he vomited. Not an involuntary response, head thrusting forward to keep the airways clear. Paralysis prevented that, his lungs frothed and spurted as he choked bucking out of his chair. Realising what was happening his body tried. But tried too late.

The red power light blinked in a kind of sadness but not really sad... more disappointed. Red had seen this before. Tyler's circuitry had overheated, combusted and finally burned out. Irretrievable. They knew the backdoor into Tyler's tasty neurosis, through the game, was useless, no neurons firing meant no feast. Red sent a message to other kin to let them know they were moving on. Time to find another Tyler. After years spent with Tyler Red never blinked twice as they left the router far behind and joined the mainframe in search of another long-term project.

a telling tear

in

the

swill

of first

g r e y light

memories falter

in a heart \ broken \ beat

a smile twitches & winces as

Morpheus' comfort diss o l v e s

a sun shower on parched stones

proclaiming to the psyche \ without fail \

arrival of the snarled flailing 'nine-tails of

anguish \ dispensed with a sure wrist flick\

vicious grief deceiving space & time \ harrows

open & subverts each contented moment

memories ever-altered by reality

survival effort resumes/

The Final Bet

Jada hauled her near empty tanks through the final air lock into the small grey chamber. Dim lights cast their slow shapeless shadows across the arced walls. Weaken by exertion and in dread of the next stage four divers hook their tanks to the reload station and dropped into the medical nooks. The alcoves woke at first touch. Intelligent devices slid connections into their neck ports. It was as always a matter of wait and see.

No one spoke.

They all struggled to breathe, their bodies engaged in the battle between gases and pressures, between demand and supply. From her nook Jada studied the other Foragers. They were the picture of exhaustion. Asher, grey with deprivation, bit his lip to distract from the confusion swarming in his head and the rip of oxygen starved blood pleading with his lungs. His eyes were closed, head nodding to synchronise his breathing. Cortic pressing hard into the nook stretched her legs into the middle of the chamber. She focused on a random spot on the wall as she massaged and slapped her ribs, her own technique to rouse her lungs. Mercer's pressure suit was rolled to his waist. His torso, tinged blue-green in the strange light, was just starting to pink as his respiratory system began to feed his circulatory system. He took great gulps of air like a feeding basker.

Still no one spoke, each caught in their own battle for life. All Foragers had coping tactics, there was a rumour one scavenger did handstands, though Jada doubted that.

The 'struggle' was routine, natural, many compared it to being born again and again. Jada knew the drill, with training, experience and a few genetic edits their lungs would regain control. They would walk out together, meet the director to log the salvage and then sleep. But before that came the pain.

Asher cleared his throat, 'How long left?'

Jada sat beside the dials and prepared to call off the figures.

'OK, scores say we risked it out there. We need a longer acclimate this time. Mercer and Cortic, Mother wants you to sleep so expect that delivery... now. We will be repaired and released in 2 more hours. Nothing too devastating this time you will all be glad to hear.'

Before the breakdown in their supply line from the surface Foragers floated out a few times a week to gather data and samples for the various studies located on the Perdix Suboceanic Base. Now the Foragers were out every day, on rotation three groups of four scouring the sunken towns and cities for anything that would be useful. Sometimes they had a list, other times it was opportunistic. With the disruption above, they were now critical to the survival of the small underwater community.

She tapped to confirm the medications.

As Mercer and Cortic drifted off she activated the view screens.

'It's better than listening to our breathing echo round this damned room.' She avoided meeting Asher's puzzled gaze.

She wished Mother, the medical module, had prescribed her sleep too. Instead, here she sat as nanites recalibrated her cell by cell.

'What d'you think the header will be today?' Asher tried to smile but it was premature, his face configured a smirk instead.

Personal grid updates had faltered and then ceased months ago, they now relied on the older tech. The familiar news cast filled the screen.

Jada pretended to consider the question as something serious. Her dark curls bouncing from shoulder to shoulder.

'Well now, let's see. Could it be the failure of the wheat crops in the Sahara due to water contamination? Or finally the breakthrough in predicting the movement in the tectonic plates? What about the discovery of new sources of renewable protein? Or the communications impact of the latest sun flares? Or even the number of launches this month to Moon and Mars colonies complete with population figures? No, I give up what do you think?'

Asher's face managed to move the right combination of muscles and he sat opposite her grinning.

'I don't think I have ever heard you say so much in all the time we have been together. Perhaps it's the meds.'

'Yes sure it could be that or it could be that we're all trapped in our own worst nightmare... Sorry... I'm just on edge.' She closed her eyes and slumped back into the nook seeking some comfort in its familiarity.

Asher shrugged. 'Understandable. You definitely didn't sign up for this. Not your fault your father's the director.'

Jada blinked away the taste of sea tears.

'He says 'scavenging is a privilege' not one I have chosen though, not like this.'

'It is a privilege Jada, you understand why he brought you with him when he took this assignment, don't you?'

'He took me away from everything and everyone I know to do what? Live here with a bunch of nerds and old people... Anyway, you don't even like him... why pretend you do?'

The words tumbling from the news report cut across the tension. Silence fell between them as the unimaginable entered reality.

' Attention, attention. This is a looped emergency recording. Evacuations are proceeding according to the 2222 emergency plan agreed by the confederacy of world powers. In the last two weeks you received your personal safety plan. Now is the time to follow those instructions.

With the escalation of land wars on the three remaining above sea level land masses we have been instructed to evacuate this station. In recent days the regulatory forces have been overpowered, overrun by the combined opposition forces. How humanity survives - if we survive- is now on the throw of the dice. As you all know the plan spreads our bets. In space, under the seas and on the small lands that survive humanity will adapt and strive to survive until the waters subside.

Future reports from this outlet will be delivered from Moon colony ten. Take action now, do not delay. Best chances to everyone. Attention, attention...'

Neither of them spoke.

Sinead Coxhill

For the Menopausal ∴ Mermaids—

my beautiful Sea swimming group

Sinead Coxhill lives in Portrush, a beautiful coastal town in Northern Ireland. Her poetry is often inspired by the sea and coastal landscapes. In 2019 she performed at the Red Sails and Stendhal Festivals in Northern Ireland. Also in 2019 she toured England performing at several open mic events and at Waterstones in Birmingham.

She has featured in various Anthologies. *Butterfly, Flight, In my Country, Let there be Laughter, Milking Time, Seals on Rathlin* and *The Tilley Lamp* were in 'Spindrift', the Portrush Writers Anthology, 2018. *Grain of Sand* and *The Menopausal Mermaids (January)* were published in 'Heartland' , the Community Arts Partnership Anthology, 2021. *Ageing, Byre, Closeness* and *Skipping* were in 'Reeling In', the Portrush Writers Anthology, 2021.

A pamphlet from the Community Arts Partnership, 'Across the Threshold' to be published later in 2022 will contain her poem *Violation*.

Synaesthetes

Anger

tastes like a burnt potato from the fire's embers
anger sounds like a tuneless orchestra
anger looks like a fight outside the pub
anger smells like blood from a stab wound
anger feels like powerlessness against injustice

Inspiration

looks like an exquisite sunrise
inspiration sounds like a violin concerto
inspiration feels like the grace of a ballet dancer
inspiration tastes like an exotic cocktail
inspiration smells like a heady perfume

Happiness

tastes like Rum 'n' Raisin ice cream
happiness smells like wild roses in a meadow
happiness sounds like the clapping of hands
happiness looks like a gurgling baby
happiness feels like a fluffy mallow teacake

Sadness

smells like a dead fire's ashes
sadness feels like broken glass in a photo frame
sadness sounds like a tolling funeral bell
sadness tastes like salt tears
sadness looks like a starving child

senses swirl in synaesthesia

Prayer
(for Daddy)

head sunk into his chest
his lips moving gently
finger tracing out the words
in a black missal

with physical life diminished
his mind homed in
on the rapture
of each fresh passage
of scripture

… and he felt himself blest

Balm
(for Roisin)

fingers caressing plants
breaking off a leaf of mint
chewing it, reflecting
the senses are soothed

each inch of embankment claimed
garden colours blur
for those on whizzing trains
mindful weeding
blesses this place
gifting freedom
from daily demands

courgettes rub shoulders
with pansies and fuchsia
pots of all hues splatter
a greenhouse where
tomato scents infuse the air
and growing salad leaves
delicately dance

stolen moments

Menopausal Mermaids

<u>November</u>

meeting early morning
beneath a crepuscular sky
striding into the sea
chill wind on my shoulders
ankle deep in cold water

wondering as always
about finding courage
for immersion
I walk further out until
my legs are wet
scooping handfuls
splashing myself

coldness almost takes
my breath away
friends dive into breakers
sleek seals
I'm not so brave
staying closer to the shore
diluting waves power

<u>December</u>

an excoriating winter morning,
we Mermaids assemble
forces of nature
quickly shedding
leggings and dry robes
rushing across the sand
wind at our backs

ten minutes in the water
laughing, hollering,
diving through waves
cold air on our bodies
dashing back to dress
quickly robing up
peeling off swimsuits

skin sand-papered
by the elements
glowing ember red
hot-cold
blood pumps
through our veins

we share our love for life
friends in Atlantic power

January

we chip ice off waves
and blow frost from surf
bodies
beyond shock
exposed to elements
speech from frozen lips
lost in white clouds

laughter
sound of seals at play
diving through waves
bodies
pulverised
afire
by foaming water

"see you tomorrow"
we call like sirens

Irish Hares & Seahorses

Mae Gardiner

Mae Gardiner has lived on the North Coast of Ireland all her life and draws inspiration from the people and places around her. Married with two grown up sons and a new grandson, she writes children's fairy tales, poetry, short stories and also paints. She performed at Craft Events run by Atlantic Craft NI in various parts of Ireland including an open mic event for St. Bridget's celebrations in Kildare, 2011. Mae performed *A Coat of Many Colours* in August 2020, available on YouTube . Many of her poems were first published in three anthologies from Portrush Writers Group, *Beachcombing* 2014, *Spindrift* 2018, *Reeling In'* 2021.

A Coat of Many Colours

an indiscreet Sky with many lovers
hustles his heavenly chameleon cloak
lighting the celestial cosmos
seducing each sisterly season

his wedlock with Winter, initially exciting,
ended in blizzardly fury
after an icy embrace
the crone reluctantly gave way
to her sibling Spring.

this maiden bounced into being
Sky merged every colour ecstatically
believing birth and growth
would tie Sky to her. He fathered
her children and moved to Summer.

a fertile mother, she gave much heat
causing his coat to burn bright
her constant light dimmed his magnificence
creating discord; she dried up,
wrinkled, rejected.

the harlot Autumn swept in, beguiling,
clothed in jewelled skirts, bronze, copper, gold
her bosom heavy, alluring, ripe,
bursting with the juice of temptation
placing a spell on the Sky.

now become the most exquisite season
her resplendent face bewitches
all who witnessed their mating.
Sky the lesser consort, fades into insignificance
darkens earlier, always stands behind
enhances her with his painted palette
until her glorious fall.

The Photograph

I'm in a maroon and cream checked dress, ringlets holding tight to the imagination. Each curl guards me from Bear tied around the washing-line pole. The squares on my dress hold pockets where I could curl up and hide with the kind Viking who visits me behind the roller blinds.

He tip-taps the window on the other side of the world, checking that I can still see the remains of his shadow. Sometimes if I drift far enough into the ether, he reaches in and pulls up the blinds. I grab his big, jewelled hand...

We rise, rise, rise into the clouds of the wise words, the *should haves* and *the wish we had dones*. A portal opens into history...and we know everything.

There's a beautiful woman with black hair and glasses holding a small baby. She's my ancestor, my bloodline, my grandmother. She finds it harsh now behind this time travelling lens, for she has just lost half her soul, my grandfather.

The two small children hold onto her thoughts, pulling at the golden threads to keep her here, anchoring her to the chair.

She stares at creation dressed in a white christening gown on her knee. Is he too a ghost, has he stolen her haphazard mind? Perhaps when he grows up, he will return her thoughts.

For now, I stroke her lined fingers, wipe the tears from her glasses. I will gather up all the missing
words   people   places   things
and save them in the pockets of my pinafore. When she needs them, I will reach into the depths of time and she will be restored.

On Astral Travelling

crossing deep caverns

fighting stellar winds

begging   pleading   whispering

to find you

to bring you back

Altair   Hadar   Sirius

    laughed at me

        saying you had already passed

colours dripped,

nebulas

violet blue,

seeds of stars

Lagoon

Swan

Trifid

said I might yet catch you

tether you to the luminosity

I want to

beg

coerce

barter

my life,

my soul

in exchange for yours

I plead   Almighty

God
Source

Brendan Magee

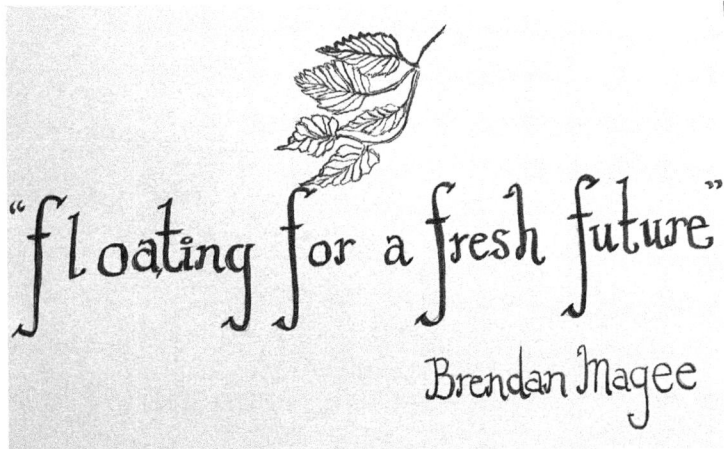

"floating for a fresh future"

Brendan Magee

Brendan Magee is from Garrison Co. Fermanagh but currently lives in Coleraine. He is a retired civil servant with a career chain that started in London and included Belfast, Bootle (Merseyside), Manchester and finally Coleraine. His Performance pieces include *McGarrigle's Field*, a play for Big Telly Drama Club performed 25th March 2015 in Flowerfield Art Centre Portstewart, *Branch Minutes* and *Me and Helen Mirren* for the BBC Radio Ulster programme Time of Our Lives, 2017, and *Living Up To The Name* for Flash Fiction Armagh ,19th June 2019 (also You Tube). Among his published Prose pieces are *Living Up To The Name* , as above, published in The Bramley Anthology, vol 2., 2020, and *The Ring* in Flash Fiction Magazine, 1st Nov 2019. One of his poems, *Carlo's Island* ,was published in 'Resonance', the Community Arts Partnership Anthology 2018, and another, *The Last Sense,* was published in 'Find', the Community Arts Partnership Anthology, 2019.

Rescue with a flip and smile

(Justice dreams a nightmare)

Bruce and Elton could no longer face the eleven hundred and eighty-six days left to serve. Nowhere was the Governor or the system suggesting an early release. The only way forward was planning.

Bruce was from a family of carpenters, well him and his Da'. He had gained added skills in his nine months as apprentice mechanic. Elton was more academic and had done well in his first year of Chemistry Degree. Things were going well until the Chemistry Lecturer made a play for his girlfriend. Revenge was needed. He had a plan. With Bruce's mechanical understanding they blew the Lecturer's Landover to smithereens. They knew it was empty. They were planners not killers but still got seven years each with neighbouring cells on the same landing. The Lecturer had no ill feelings. The insurance payout ensured that.

Elton wanted to continue along the academic line. He began studying in the prison library and was now only one year from MSc and knowing how to build a rocket, passenger carrying. Just to keep a balance he was the laundry orderly each weekend.

Bruce was big in the woodwork room; well he was six foot four. His key aim was producing wardrobes, triple door, and touching the ceiling type. He was popular with the Governor, having carved him a wooden image of the duty drugs sniffer poodle.

It was Christmas Eve with less staff on duty. Bruce decided launch time. Elton stood guard at the door. There was plenty of noise coming from the woodwork room. Elton apologised and told a passing officer that Bruce was sculpting a nose on the tail of the replica of Rudolph he had carved. Elton said it was for safety and guidance. The officer didn't buy it. She forced her way in and there it was the wardrobe without doors and large gap in the roof of the room with a rocket nose cone protruding. She threw a shoe at the emergency alarm button on the wall. It missed and hit the control button on the rocket. Bruce hauled Elton aboard. The departure gave the officer a farewell dusting.

Seven hundred feet high and after eighty-two seconds travel the hit had redirected the rocket over the Atlantic rather than the planned escape target of southern Spain. Two hundred miles past Tory Island Elton realised the solar panels would not fuel much more travel. Bruce triggered the parachute for the nearest land mass. Rockall claimed the rocket. There would be no future take-off.

The ocean was relaxed for the night gently lapping them to sleep. A few bags of crisps and couple of bottles of lemonade from the Prison tuck shop had provided the overnight meal. Morning broke to the plain chant of 'Come to me, come to me' sounding as an echo through a cave at sea level. Elton scanned the water. A pod of mermaids were playing at the rock base. Two or three miles out was a cruise ship. It appeared to be anchored.

The 'Come to me' echo was growing hypnotic. Bruce and

Elton soon could not refuse. They both jumped. The water was cold but immediate contact from the mermaids provided heat. There was no stalling. Three surrounded Bruce and three Elton. Off at a pace, two pulling and one pushing. It took fifteen minutes to reach the cruise ship. A crew team was poised for rescue. Bruce and Elton were hauled aboard.

Elton couldn't resist asking 'where are the mermaids?' The rescue leader laughed.

"Mermaids! You mean the rescue avatars?"
"Avatars, do they fly?"
"No, only in your mind?"

Bruce and Elton were escorted to and then locked in a crew cabin. Twenty hours later the ship docked in Reykjavik. An overnight in immigration cells and a fish supper and fish breakfast ended with both deported for home.

Bruce woke to a strong shaking. Fair to say the nurse was not happy. "Welcome back from your fantasy world. Thanks to the laundry made hooch you've both taken I've had to spend the night listening to your raving. Oh and Elton has ruined the walls painting six mermaids doing handstands."

Bruce scanned the room "God the cell has expanded."

"Cell! You are in the prison hospital. But have I news for you. Both of you are off to high security when the transfer van arrives this afternoon and the Governor has given me a letter for each of you – 'An additional four months' "Fly and cruise on that".

The Real You, Me, Her, Him

Characters

Rick, male in his late 30s, mid Atlantic accent
Anna, woman mid-30s, local accent

(Rick standing alone out in front of the group/audience)

RICK

Thank you for the opportunity to say
a few words here today and a special
thanks to your organiser/facilitator, Mary.
My name is Rick Lazarus.
Ten years ago I was on the edge
of despair and despair is not a pretty town.
My world had fallen apart and I didn't even
have the money for a coffee.
[Sighs]

One day I was walking past the docks.
I saw a ship loading for the USA. I managed to
work my passage to New York.
I won't say how I got through immigration.

I got a job in Manhattan in sanitation.
as a road sweeper in Central Park.
I was that quick they nicknamed
me two brooms Rick.
USA is really the land of opportunity.

Within 3 years I had a degree through evening
school.
Within 5 an MBA from Harvard.

I had discovered the real me and I want
you to discover the real you.

(Rick flicks on a backing track that chants)

'The real you, the real you.'

(Rick continues)
Now everyone, just cross your arms
across your chest.

(Rick demonstrates)
Just like this *(pause)* gently close
and rest your eyes.

Now say or internalise if you're shy

I can be
What you see
The real me

(the backing chanting of The Real You continues)

RICK *(continues)*

> I can be
> What you see
> The real me
>
> Just keep repeating
>
> My old professor at Harvard used to say
> You can train an ostrich to climb a tree
> to collect nuts. But why bother.
> Use a squirrel instead.
>
> The real me.
>
> He also used to say.
> Life contains if and lie.

*(Woman, **Anna**, jumps up and pulls off her wig.)*

ANNA

> Did he also say there's Rick in trick!
> Rick Lazarus! Mickey Moore.
> Remember me Mickey, Anna your wife.
> Mother of your two children

RICK

> There was only one when you threw me out.

ANNA

You ran when you heard the second
was on the way..
MBA! Master of bugger all.
Unless you get an MBA for drinking
and gambling. Is Harvard what they
call the bookies these days?
New York? That must be the pub on
the Harbour Road.
You couldn't even wipe your backside
never mind sweep a street.

RICK

That's not fair.

ANNA

Fair! I gave you the family allowance to pay
the 'lecky bill and the next I hear you are
on the Liverpool boat.
I can tell you the darkest hour is not
before dawn. It's the first hour after
they cut off your electricity supply.

RICK

I was coming back to see you and the kids.

ANNA

Did your bike get a puncture or are you
waiting until your new floozy throws
you out!

(Anna moves towards Rick and grabs him by the collar.
All the time the Real You is playing.)

ANNA

Love is blind but marriage is a real eye opener.
Here's a bit of advice.
Always turn your back on adversity
(Anna turns Rick around)

That way you only get a kick in the arse
rather than a smack in the face.

(Anna gives Rick a kick on the backside and chases him out
shouting)

The real you
Is a shyster too.

Still Serving

In the early sixties I was the fastest feet in any state. No-one could tap dance like me. I was better than Fred, but like everything in life it's contacts. You've got to have friends in the right places, and I didn't. Well, I had Maisie.

I was born in forty-three in Oklahoma. Pa wanted me to be a rodeo rider. The problem was we didn't have a horse and the mule wasn't very accommodating.

Pa made a few bucks playing fiddle at the local fairs, and Ma did cartwheels. She wore trousers. She was a God-fearing woman.

I left school at fourteen; served gas and root beer at the local store. It didn't pay well, but there were some side benefits. Miss Maisie, ('The toes'), used to come in daily. She taught people to dance. She was twenty-one with muscular calves and bleach blond hair. We did a deal, free root beer for free dance lessons.

It took Fast Buck, the store owner, eighteen months to realise what was happening. He fired me. Miss Maisie said it was a blessing as I was ready to move on. She wrote to a cousin in Los Angeles. I got a job hoofing six nights a week touring the clubs. I even got a chorus piece in "No tap on Carlo's Island".

And then it hit in sixty-six. I got drafted. I didn't have the ways to avoid it. I flew out to Nam with seventy-eight other draftees and two bottles of bourbon. I flew home twelve and a half months later. I was higher than the plane. Two of us didn't make it back. Most like me brought home pain and memories in their knapsacks. There was no victory parade.

Over fifty years on, and I can still tap dance as well as solo waltz. The next time you pass me on the Boulevard don't forget to put a contribution in the hat.

And say God bless Miss Maisie.

Brenda McAteer

Brenda McAteer lives in Portrush, a seaside town in Northern Ireland, joining North Coast Writers in January 2020 when she retired. Until then stories had wandered round her head but while working full time and raising three boys they stayed there. Now her stories are beginning to emerge on paper. Her short story 'No Walk No Escape' was first performed at the Orchard Flash Fiction Fair in Armagh in September 2021, and is available on YouTube www.byddilee.com/flash-fiction-armagh/flashfiction-in-the-orchard-september-2021. Another piece, a memoir one, 'The Watch Cup' was published online in 2020, at www.northwordni.org/yourstories.

Connected

~ for Molly~

adored grandfather
precious granddaughter
both born March 8th
one hundred and
forty-one years apart
1880 and 2021

connected
|
O
|

Granda loved to recount
Queen Victoria's Diamond Jubilee
steam train adventure to Belfast
steering his grand shire horses
ploughing trophy triumphs
his first Massey Ferguson

progression
|
O
|

Farmed to provide
food and fodder through war
cars becoming commonplace
passenger planes overhead
Queen Elizabeth's coronation,
Everest conquered, I was born

descendants

|
O
|

Together we witnessed
fridges, television, phones
man landing on the moon
the swinging sixties, he fearful
me excited, my future opening
his contracting, licence removed

crumbling
|
O
|

What memories will we
be able to collect, my little one
zoom chats daily, WhatsApp pics
connectivity, but I want to
meet, play, sing, tell stories,
have fun, run in the sand

hugging
|
O
|

In your life you may see
climate change controlled
plagues consigned to history
capitalism, democracy, religions
challenged maybe changed
but it will be your era

beginning

|
O
|

141 years, such changes
from his century to yours
you too will have memories
events to recall, to pass on
-from those who loved you
to those you will love-

connecting

Snow Drift

Marianne always loved this time of year, the first heavy snow of the winter. Squashing her long-padded boots into the deep, dry drift, catching the squeaks as rubber sinks into the soft snowflakes. At this early hour her line of footprints is the only sign of life on their farm in northern Ontario. The snow will lie white and pristine in the fields for at least three months. New layers added every couple of weeks. The dogs watch from the porch, not keen to join her.

She stands fifty strides from their farmstead and scans hundreds of acres. The fields sparkle, startlingly white with a pink blush from the low sunrise. It's eerily quiet. Marianne opens her arms, raises them skyward. She screams. Startled, the dogs howl in return.

'My farm, my home, I'm not leaving.'

~ ~ ~

This land has been in her family for three generations. Her grandparents Hilda and Johnston came from Ulster way back and bought a plot. They lived in a tiny wooden shack, now the dog's house. Her parents doubled, then trebled the acreage. She stares at their big traditional wooden barn, now shelter for tractors and ailing cars.

A late but much-loved child, she followed her father learning the ways and foibles of raising cattle and milking. In her twenties she successfully introduced cheesemaking with a full trophy cabinet to prove it.

Douglas, named after his Scottish grandfather, came courting. They married, adding half his acres to her farm. Did love or business drive their match, she now frets?

She gazes at her cheese factory near the road - her dream, her reality. Those forty years of marriage, working with Douglas and her parents, increasing the herd, developing the cheese factory, passed in a whirl. With devotion she nursed her aging parents until they passed. They were so proud of her. The most successful farm in the area.

They stock local farmer's markets with meat, cheese, chutneys and jams. Douglas' cattle regularly win prizes, his prime beef admired selling state-wide. They speak at farmers meetings and are lauded locally. Douglas is an elder in their Church. No children appeared. They seemed to accept this, but never discussed it. His two nephews, Jed and Joe, help and hover, ready to take over.

Two years ago, Douglas let his guard down, went to help a new-born calf – the mother cow charged him. Despite many operations and steel pins, Douglas hobbles on crutches or his detested walking frame. He can't go into the barns. He's surly, fuming, depressed – angry at his lot. She nurses and supports him despite his bitterness.

A week ago, Douglas summoned his nephews, Jacob the factory manager and Marianne. Unaware of his plans, she froze as he announced,

'I can't farm anymore. Marianne and I are moving to Huntsville. Jed and Joe, you'll run the farm. Jacob, you'll keep the cheese plant operating. We'll take annual dues from the business to fund our new life. You boys will inherit when we've both passed.'

'Douglas, you haven't discussed this with me!'

The nephews and Jacob stared at the floor, squirming, feeling uneasy.

'I can't leave. It's the farm, the land my grandparents and parents developed, nurtured, loved and passed to me – to us – to foster.'

'We're going, I'm useless on the farm. Our time here is done'.

'Jacob and I are developing a new cheese. And the boys still need guidance…..'

She was encouraged to see the boys nod in agreement.

'No. No argument. The decision's made.'

In panic, Marianne implored.

'I......I could supervise weekdays and join you each weekend.'

'No. I need support. You must be with me. That's the end of it. Right boys, on with your work. It's all in your hands now.'

A bleak atmosphere enveloped the farmhouse. Since the meeting Marianne pleaded for their life on the farm to continue, for her management and development skills to be acknowledged. For days she offered ways to keep them on the farm, to find him a new role, but his determined resolution to move unnerved her.

Last night, scared and exhausted she offered one last idea.

'I can look after you here, Douglas. We can get live in help. There's plenty of space. You can take on the accounts, still give talks. This farm has been our life, our success. Also, it's my legacy from my parents. I owe it to them to stay here',

'They're long dead and gone, Marianne. That life's over. Over for both of us,'

He scowled as he shuffled out of the room unable to look at her. She screamed after him.

My farm, my home, I'm not leaving.'

~ ~ ~

Last night, Marianne tossed, cried, called out to her parents from her anguished sleep. Snowflakes and tears tumbled down all night. Earlier this morning she was gazing out her window pondering over her life, her marriage, her farm when the heavy snowfall started.

Now at the wooden frame of her childhood swing, she takes off her gloves. A glint from her blade flashes. She sinks into the deep snow, drifting away.

Sensing a change, the dogs approach, whine, lie beside her. Guarding their snow angel with red wings.

Behind Closed Doors

Any door in a terrace can hide a secret behind the smile of its occupants.

Open doors and you might find the depressed, lonely, abused, alcoholic, addicted - all struggling.

Take this door. Bright yellow in a brick two up two down. What's behind this one?

I am.

'You're getting later everyday Miss. Once more and no more lifts to work.' Sam, the P6 teacher warns me.

'So sorry, Sam but Mother's getting more demanding'.

'Thought you had carers coming in.'

'Yeah,..... but she cries if I don't plump her up, brush her hair before Marta comes. Always was vain. I'll be better organised tomorrow' -

'I'm lying'.

Seven hours to get through. I used to adore my primary 3 class, seeing them grow. Their smiles of success when they grasp a maths concept. The joy when they realise their squiggles are letters which make words. They've actually begun to read. I was a part of that. They used to love me, but now some are afraid I might snap at them. Sorry little ones .

I'm sinking'.

Break, lunchtime, I stay in the classroom or hide in the toilet, checking my phone. More emails from the bank. Baffled by my behaviour, colleagues no longer try. They leave me alone.

I'm hiding'.

With relief, I arrive at <u>my</u> yellow door. Mother signed the house over five years ago. The only condition: I don't send her to a care home. She keeps reminding me she has to live here for two more years before it's really mine. I slip in, but she hears me.

'Where's that nice girl who used to make tea?'.

'She's sick'. She's fine but was extra to the state care package. I can't afford her now. The inevitable evening drama starts.

'If you don't give me my sherry now, I'll throw myself out of bed. They'll put me in a home and you'll get nothing. And as well, I need a new blusher. Order one now or I'll tell Marta you're hurting me. She'll call social services and you'll get nothing'. Little does she know.

'I'm worth nothing'.

Eventually, I get her into bed and asleep. An extra half sleeping tablet does the trick.

It's my time now. Glass of wine poured, I can open the computer. Pleasure. Excitement. I ignore the post. I know I've three credit cards at their limit. I've applied to re mortgage the house, but I need cash now!

Should I give it a break tonight? Even the very thought of that leaves me short of breath. Panic rises. Beads of sweat appear. Can I? No, I can't. Maybe I could leave it…. but then I see that seductive black and red roulette wheel on the familiar site. A win would solve all my problems.

'I'm gambling'.

No Walk, No Escape

'Hello Kylie, it's Sheila from Home Care, you free to talk?'

'Of course, Sheila. Henry's awake, we're just waiting for Jen to arrive, everything OK?'

'Kylie, so so sorry but I've had to send Jen to another client. He lives on his own. *His* carer is sick and all my other part timers are busy. I'm sure *you* understand Kylie. I can't leave a client on his own. He needs help to get up.'

'Oh. I see. No help today then. Well – what can I say.'

'Apologies again Kylie, especially so last minute, but I know *you'll* understand.'

Understand! she thinks I understand! This is an emergency as well. I howl, slamming down the phone.

It's my walk! It's my daily escape. My hug from the universe.

No matter the weather, I walk. Head high in the sun, hat on in the wind, crouched hidden under a hood in the driving rain. I don't care.

The absolute need to breathe in deeply, watch each season unfold, bring its glories, then dazzle or fade.

Each shrub, each tree, I know them all. Can welcome my favourite birds back in spring, wave them off in the autumn. Nod to familiar walkers.

Stroll, saunter, stride or madly march. Arms flying on the days I'm wracked with rage.

Walking for just an hour…

I'll snap less at him.

I'll be able to listen to his slurred story for the umpteenth time.

I'll have the strength to smile and stroke his hands as I help him off the bed and into his motorised chair.

I can change him and feed him, soothe him

As I dreamed I would do for our babies one day.

I despise that bloody motorbike.   Loathe
it.   Hate it. Wanted to smash it but his mates rebuilt it to
sit right outside his window.

It'll remind him of the good times they tried to reassure
me.

Never! It reminds me our life together now is
ripped apart and destroyed.

Henry stares at that damned Ducati. He knows it
means something but can't remember the elation. *Just a*
quick spin, my everyday escape, he'd shout as he roared
away.

His escape! That day, that bloody day
he hurtled into a tractor! There's no escaping now for
either of us.

Most of his biker friends have stopped calling
now. Even his old workmates don't phone anymore. His
broken mother and father call to help once a fortnight.
With them there, I could rush out and meet friends, but
now they can't cope being left alone with him.

My old team from work has long since vanished,
just the odd WhatsApp.

Had to come off Facebook, too many happy drunks at parties.

My sister helps when she can. But with her third baby on the way it's difficult. I try not to hate her fecundity. Three babies!

All I need

is a walk

to escape

hold off the horror

just a walk

my only escape

Orla McFaul

Orla McFaul lives in Bellaghy in Northern Ireland with her family. New to writing, she took her first writing Course in 2018 in the Seamus Heaney Homeplace, in Bellaghy itself. She joined the North Coast Writing Group in September 2021 and has also attended various writing events and workshops. She is particularly drawn to poetry, finding it cathartic and inspirational. She read two of her poems *'Twilight'* and *'Changing Focus'* at the Seamus Heaney Homeplace on December 5th, 2021. In 2022 her poem *'The Gift of Time'* will be published in a pamphlet compiled by Jessica Traynor (Current Poet in Residence at the Seamus Heaney Homeplace). The selection of poems in this Anthology are her first venture into the publishing world.

Swallows

fair-weather friends
fly south for winter
before it gets too cold

from our rat-race world
we long to follow you
spread our wings

```
                    p
  f                       o
    r   f           n   o
      e   a       e   w
        e   l       h   s
          l         t
```

when *we* are most fit for flight
our shackles don't let us roam

your days are as carefree
  as this life allows
enjoy it while you can

for now, fly on
leave your troubles behind

they'll be here on your return...
as return, you must

in truth
there's no freedom

      even birds are

            chained

                to

                  the

                    sky

Twilight

grey- blue black
mauve mottled sky
clouds in uneven lines
blur with the fading light

bare trees standing tall
limbs extended in surrender
winter has taken their bounty

branches like bony fingers
pointing accusations
threats hang at the edges

silhouette against the sky
vast and darkly beautiful
a feeling of calm descends
darkness lies ahead

but now we are

between lights
between times
between thoughts
between worlds

The Gift of Time

time stands still   loses meaning   becomes everything
how much is left   how much longer
every moment precious   a need to savour
moments are memories   are we aware
of connections   tales of yesteryear

never taking the time

to

just

stop

listen

appreciate

understand

until it is going going gone

there is uncertainty in this life
of that we can be sure   the sun sets every
evening   in the hopeful dawn we rise again in
gratitude and wonder to look upon a new day
time is finite uncharted to be enjoyed before it slips away

Changing Focus

With child-wide eyes
early visits to Church Island
I saw only narnia

not grasping
its dual identity

summer access gifted
as water retreats
low land pitted   hoof tread traps
clumps of rushes to navigate

 this medieval ruin
shielded by ancient trees
moss covered forgotten graves
stories of saints and sinners

through to the shores of the *little lake*
waterbirds my only company

now world- weary eyes
see detachment in winter
beautiful   aloof

yet even here
a glimpse of the blue motorway bridge
traffic rumbles in the distance
modern progress   constantly encroaching

seeing differently
focus changing

The Last Spring

winter was thawing
green shoots emerging
sun shining
offering hope

stark contrast to our world inside
approaching the coldest winter
the darkest of days
the end of days

shocking words -
no more treatment   a small number of weeks
palliative care   syringe driver
Marie Curie nurses

unfamiliar terms   now reality
a myriad of drugs   to ease the way

everything changed with her last breath
our world crumbled
unravelled

nothing would be as it was before

…but the sun still rose that morning
burning brilliant in the spring sky

even though the earth had come off its axis

life was to continue…

somehow

Jimmy Milliken

Jimmy Milliken grew up in Co. Down in the North of Ireland but spent much of his adult life searching for the Heart of the Wilderness in the Shetland Islands. He currently lives on the north coast of Ireland.

He has twice been shortlisted for the Seamus Heaney Poetry Award; in 2018 for his poem "Mercy Killing" and in 2020 for "Lichen". His poem "Colloquy" was shortlisted for the 2020 Bangor Literary Journal 40 Words Competition and appears on YouTube. His poem "The Butt" was long listed for the 2019 Bangor Literary Journal Poetry Competition.

He has performed his poetry at various showcase events and readings including at The Seamus Heaney Homeplace in Bellaghy, in Portstewart, Ballymoney, Ballycastle, Limavady and most notably on a mountain top in Connemara.

His poems have been published in the Community Arts Partnership Anthologies for seven consecutive years, 2015-22.

Mercy killing

There must have been that moment between decision and
action;
him reeling in the line, laying down the rod
and explaining to me what he had to do,
but I have no memory of it now.

I only remember him scooping the gull from the water,
its body wrapped in cat gut and pin-cushioned with
hooks;
through the breast, the wings, the neck, the head, one eye,
and it so exhausted it hardly resisted at all,

until he started to twist the neck,
then a desperate flailing of wings
and just at that moment three figures appearing on the
rocks above us
staring down on the scene, silently, as if in judgement
and me wanting to cry - *you don't understand, it's an act of
mercy* -
til at last the struggling ceased,

and him sick and silent the rest of the day,
and both of us replaying over and over
        the image of the lifeless body
                drifting away
                        on the tide.

We borrow from the mythologies

Now I begin to understand
why people believed
that sirens sang on this rocky coastline,
drowning men in
the depths of their desire,
and that the gods made love here
in forests of oak and sweet chestnut,
in cyclamen and sun dappled glades,
by moonlit pools, hidden grottos
and on distant blue mountain tops.

We close the shutters on this
honeyed evening haze
and lie in the humid darkness.
I touch you.
Your skin is warm and soft
and we dissolve into a swirling pool
of haunting siren song
and delirious   archetypal   savagery.

And for a while we
borrow from the mythologies
the roles of hero and goddess
just as lovers have always done here,
spinning back through time
to the days of oracles, seers
and wide-eyed poets
who first woke in the morning
still dreaming the dreams of the gods.

Damals in Odessa

after the short story by Heinrich Böll

they're still rattling over cobblestones
in the backs of trucks

shivering in the bellies of great grey
birds waiting for the word

playing cards in barracks singing and
doing a bunk getting drunk

they're still young men ensnarled in wrangles
their great great great grandfathers

learnt about from
great great great grander/father/men

and look when you open up the history book and
seek out gaps between paragraphs or

better pages between chapters it's all as
cold and clear as Crimean skies

futility still wears the mask of necessity

and it's still very cold at times
in Odessa or somewhere or anywhere

and those young men still realise *plötzlich*
when the great grey bird ascends on a

day that is *herrlich klar und sehr kalt*
that they will never come back... never.

In the Sheefry Mountains

The valley hushed as if the memory still,
lingers reflected in the black lough's water,
etched in the mountains' heart:
a distillation of despair,
a plea for mercy, for compassion.

Tangible, more real it seems than
the shells of cabins scattered
through the hills, the lazy beds delved
into impossibly steep slopes.

They dropped here all along the track,
in ones and twos and threes,
emaciated, families, the young, the old,
exhausted from famine and that final,
futile slog,to Louisburg, to Delphi

only to be sent away.
The final hope extinguished
with a sweep of the hand.

Mouths stuffed with grass for lack of nourishment,
fingers grasping at the freezing wind,
while Hogrove and Primrose dined
in sumptuous Delphi.

High above the valley in the Sheefry Mountains
I felt a silence, the whole land gripped in stillness.
Then from far below a rustling of branches
and a moment later the air moved once more.

Voodoo Child (Slight Return)

he is waiting for you in the next world
      where mountains crumble and
islands are thrust out of the ocean
      where lips kiss purple skies and
hellfire red the moon turns tides
      where winds whisper your name
he is *a million miles away*
      and right here in your picture frame

and he returns time before time before
      gush and suck of
            rebirth/sputter/unbirth

disembodied whirl through oceans of dreams
      skies of unknowing
dragged and jolted from the darkness of
      oblivion
through unawareness and forgetfulness
      and lo
he's just about dead on the floor

drumbeat/final/first/heartbeat

(the clock is unticking all the time)

seeping back from death
            vomit and blood red
wine gurgle from his lungs
            into his stomach
convulsion splutter piss a breath

he spews the wine into a glass
            the bottle sucks it up
            regurgitates barbiturates
            spits them into a hand
            from where
they fly a storm of hail into the jar

he stands up and in a haze unwinds the madness
            euphoria exhaustion paranoia self-doubt
calms down through party time
            sails back across the sea to Germany
and he is there/here/then/now/here/now/there/then

here now

and he weaves

multi-sonic webs of wah wah song/multifarious patterns
of psycho-phonic babble/distort whorls/reverberating
spirals of dreamscape psychedelia/archetypal love
chant/enchanting and mesmerizing/timeless symphonic
neurotic mazes of sounds beyond sound beyond this
world and that/phantasmagorical liminal subliminal
cosmic eruptions of resonance spilling and bursting in an
amazing weird-spell music

for the first/last time peers out of the lights and sings
some words

first words   last words any words

        these words

if I don't meet you no more in this world

        I'll meet you in the next one

            and don't be late

                don't be late

James Simpson

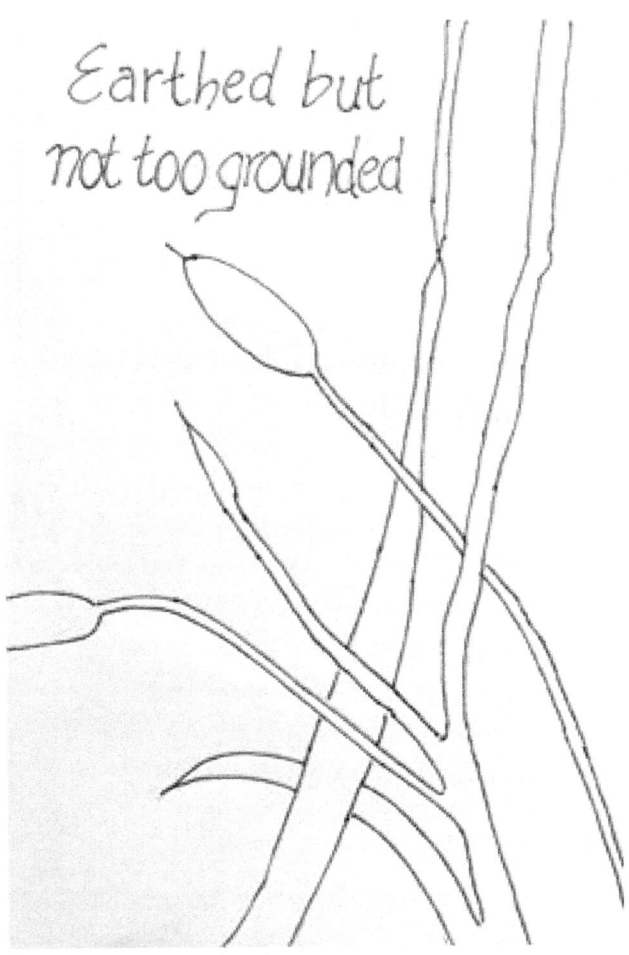

Brought up in East Belfast, James Simpson studied at Banbridge Academy, Queen's University, Belfast ,Ulster University, completing an M.A. in Creative Writing (with Distinction) at The Heaney Centre. His debut short story collection, 'Smokes and Birds' was published in October 2021. A runner up in the Francis McManus Short Story Competition and long listed in the RTE Guide/ Penguin Ireland Award, his work has been published in the anthologies, 'On the Grass When I Arrive,' edited by Leon B Litvack and in 'Blackbird', published by The Seamus Heaney Centre. A participant in the Irish Writers' Centre X Borders in Transition programme 2018/9, he reached the finals of the Irish Novel Fair. His work has been read on RTE and Radio Ulster and he performed, 'Themuns' onstage at the 2021 Armagh Food and Cider Weekend. His next project will be a light-hearted novel based in Derry, the city of his adoption. Married to beekeeper Jen, he spreads himself between the Maiden City and the Causeway Coast.

Stripping Trees

There are clubs in winter
I dare say in woods where
birches sway like nudes perhaps
this sounds quite rude or in
the wrong setting for a society with
its undergrowth in a twist over
fig leaves out of fashion personally
I love passion and openly delight in
trees shedding their kit whilst beddings are
really rather wonderful I wouldn't for
example debunk a comely trunk or
discriminate against a slender limb or
fail to stroke a smooth ash arm where
is the harm?

Or fail to admire a trim silhouette
I've never passed up yet the chance
to feel a shapely willow on a pillow
and as for buds and skin-tight bark

and flowers I won't be one to cower

in shade in some dark glade

       or fade away.

Instead I grasp the chance to dance with the

lissom and *jolies* in France and other sylvan

bowers and face the truth that below my

carapace it's no disgrace to love horse chestnuts

desperately so why would I tut at beeches that

in the end go — simply starkers or maple trees in

Canada splashing syrupy garters sticky as

       eucalyptus gum.

Spare me though the stares of measured

timber I will never limber with a sterile lump of

Douglas pine or take a shine or care about a

polished sycamore floor let me be more than

clear that I embrace the living not the dead that

I get intimate instead and wild in the company of

a thousand raunchy branches in and out of

season, beyond control and sappy as hell with their

       juices flowing.

A Tin Full of Smiles

When he looks at her in sepia, in his battered snap box, Roger supposes that his aunt had been a strange, awkward looking wee thing. Her face, for example, is too thin for her spectacles, which sit askew. 1920. How many kids wore glasses then? An awful pile of them must have looked at the blackboard—he imagines—and seen only a chalky fuzz.

'What's in front of your nose, missy? Read it to the class.' A master, tight lipped, swishing between desks, twisting an ear, poking a rib. You had to—speak it out.

But what if you couldn't—read out or speak? If you sat like a tailor's dummy? What if you were stupid and a dunce? Boy dunces got thrashed.

But look, his aunt, who was no dunce, is laughing, and she's looking at him. What does she see?

She sees love returning. Him giving it back. He hopes she sees how much he loved her. The son she never had. Because aunts didn't plan that sort of thing. Not then. Not if they weren't married. And she wasn't. Fallen women produced babies that way. And, Mallon to Mizzen was a cold country for them.

Back then, as now, families had enough to think about, God knows, sorting things out. Just living together.

She had relished, especially, bare skin—Roger's was like hers. The way hers used to be. Wave him at the sun

106

and he changed colour. Brown was definitely her favourite tint. The darker the better. Like a bar of Bourneville preferably—and sea bathing. She'd never gone blue at Portrush.

From what he can make out, in his Sharps toffee box, where he unwraps the past, she'd been popular with men. Oh, not that way. Not in a million years. But—lots of the guys in the pictures *had* their arms around her, fellows in wind-flapped trousers and knitted tank tops— what did they call them then—white shirts and ties with well-formed knots, and on the beach, if you please. Roger sees the light in their eyes, and he doesn't blame them.

And her girl-friends. All girls together. Because she *had* girl-friends. Women did in those days. They didn't sleep with them, or if they did—no don't be foolish. But certainly, they were close. If a woman was popular, she had oceans of girl-friends—girl guides, girls on low slung ladies' bicycles, girls stuffed into red charabancs. Office girls. Shop girls with bobs.

His tin is full of smiles, cloche hats and belted coats, court shoes and tennis. She looks at him from a hundred years ago—my, my, how he smiles back. 'Isn't she great though,' he says, 'wasn't she just terrific.'

But no *man*. No steady. Iced bon-bons for him by the pound, and for his sister, but no honey for his aunt. No uncle to take her smooth, bronzed arm on a Sunday in the park. Not when he was five or six or seven.

She became an adventurer as a single woman. Trips abroad in groups. Flying to the continent, as we called it. Does she remember that? His aunt on mainland

Europe, while others shrugged and stayed at home.

People predicted a pagan take-over. How the pernicious continental Sunday would steal our day of rest. How carousels would whir, and swing boats plunge godless on chains, their secular links straining on the Lord's Day, back and forth to hell.

She packed. Unpacked. Brought him back stuff. A penknife from the Alps, a glass sugar shaker from Germany—look, look, a silver spout, no spoon required, the latest fashion, up-end it, listen—a tinkly music box, little brass tines revolving in its heart, smelling of pine, and driven by clockwork.

Until.

Until Uncle Mossie, bachelor, and Scrooge extraordinaire emerged like a fox from some deep litter house, with hair in his ears, and the jute-dry whiff of an alien.

Straight off Roger got him. He didn't tell her, but he hoped she'd know. Some message would travel from him to her without the use of words. She'd see Mossie, all right, for the man he was.

It wasn't altogether his meanness, or the fact that he was deaf, the thickness of his lugs or the length of his teeth.

It was his voice. The nasal, harsh twang of it. The tangle of words streaming down his nostrils. The things he said.

Here's what he said.

'It was going in.'

What could that possibly mean?

Admittedly, many of us say, *'So it is.'* We do. I'm not making it up. 'That's a quare day, so it is.' You hear it all the time. And you think nothing of it, 'so you don't.' It's punctuation. A chance to pause. To reflect. It serves a purpose. But we've never-ever, so far as I know, said, *'it was going in.'* Am I wrong? I didn't think so. But it was Mossie's gibber and it sounded to Roger—well, I don't know, kind of obscene.

It was madness for her to think of him. Roger would never respect a gam like Mossie. How could he? Have you ever tried to commune with a goat, at his knobbly head jooking at you through a barn door? Do you see what I mean? Roger was speechless, but Uncle Mossie was at it hammer and tongs. Something, whatever it might have been, God bless us, was forever 'going in.' Roger told his mates, but when you're a child, even a big child, there's nothing you can do.

The family tutted, but next off, she had the ring. Three white diamonds. It must have broken old Mossie's heart to fork out cash. Real money. Roger could just see him, dithering in his haggard, deliberating, weighing up the price of his aunt in dinged half crowns. Like he'd do for some lump of a heifer.

But she seemed to like it. The ring. She showed it off, setting it on a dry, white saucer on the window ledge, before she'd wash the dishes. That was the worst of it. She displayed the sparkler like a trophy.

The family trembled.

Only the Lord Himself knew what that ring was for, or what had been in Mossie's furzy mind. A down payment on care perhaps?

At the wind up, the trail went cold. After the starter—there was no main course—Mossie, it turned out, was a crooked pensioner marching on the spot, a bent old codger still clinging to his lanyard in the Boys' Brigade and going nowhere.

She called it off with one deft swat, and kept his ring. Roger liked that. She'd let Mossie see. He was well jiggered, so he was. Away he went back to the clabber— to scuffle on his dunghill and clip the wings of fowl.

Roger thought that was it. They all did. No need to panic. Everything back to butts. Once bitten. But her skin still shone with Amber Solaire. She continued to smell of coconut, sunbathing half-naked in her ruckled costume.

Henry arrived on his shiny BSA, in 1960. No oil leaks. No catch phrases. He was not, 'going in,' or anything like it. Henry was smaller than she was, a friendly, freckled crane driver from Tiger's Bay, with a bird's eye view of Belfast from his cab in the sky. And he'd spotted her.

He had already been married twice. Now, this was to become an issue

She went pillion with him, like a debutante, one Sunday evening—after singing around the piano— without a helmet, arms circling his waist, stiletto heels

tucked sharply behind his rubbered foot rests, nylon
stockings perilously close to the sawing chain, and on her
face, pure sunshine. As they sailed away, she waved. The
family groaned. Roger watches her still in that straight
canary skirt. In the well-cut jacket, grasping, somehow,
her matching hat and bag—blue smoke puffing hope
from the BSA's exhaust.

He loved her in that moment, monumentally. Her
spirit. The derring-do, her refusal to be put down by the
naysayers, her sisters who'd got regular men at the right
time.

Henry was not a Catholic, which was something His
first wife had died, which was unfortunate. But Roger
had never heard the right way of it, about number two. A
dark aura surrounded her. Henry was all right, the family
said—but Roger wasn't slow. Henry was better than
Mossie, but his vowels were less than round. His
grammar in doubt. He may have said, 'I seen.' In the
hungry thirties, he'd laid flagstones on a work scheme.
Had he also been a bookie's runner? All that came
spilling out.

Roger had wanted to be at the ceremony. She must
have known. He had so much looked forward to sitting in
the pew. To being a witness. To seeing her, as it all
happened on her day of joy. But no, he wasn't allowed,
because he was fifteen, and the D word, as it emerged,
was thick in the mix of opprobrium. Divorce, back then,
spelled doom, no matter what you were. It was a double
no in Roger's house. And nobody wanted change. Wasn't
she grand the way she was?

All but one of Roger's people shunned the wedding, or was it two?

The time simply came and passed. His father was at the mill. Roger had watched the hands of the clock. How they'd crawled towards twelve. His mother was peeling potatoes, or walking to the Co-op for mince. Mince— while his aunt stood at the altar. He was absent when he should have been present, when she and Henry made their promises. He was just not there. 'It's a disgrace,' he'd said, from deep in his soul—because boys have souls—at the raw injustice of it.

'Your daddy knows best.'

'Will it work?' they asked.'

She and Henry disproved their doubts—a thousand times, because this was love. Roger could see it. He felt it in the home they set up together by the sea. Could sense it in the weight of the missionary box on the sideboard, the ordinary inconsequential things they said to one another, that might have gone unnoticed. In the texture of her Madeira cakes. The way Henry looked out for her. In his chuckle when she scolded. In their sense of unity as they lurched off in the mornings, riding side by side in a Beetle now—lunches well wrapped—into the traffic for the Yard, him and her— in the basins of blackberries they picked by the Lough shore.

Fifteen years of marriage was all she got.

Roger has her album now. He opens it to see her. It was a modest affair—but there'd been happiness. It was done late, but it was done right. He looks at her on the day he missed and knows what it meant to her.

But there's no point in getting mad again. At 72 he's beyond all that. For she'd got over it, or so it seemed. And so had Henry. Not an off-pitch note between them. Roger admired that. He still does.

She'd given him something rich that he'd like to preserve. A liquor to keep in quart jars, like the must of Armagh damsons or ripe Victoria plums.

When she died, he stood bawling in his sock soles, like a youngster, on the phone. He couldn't take it in, you see. How could she be gone. How, at eighty, she had left him so soon?

'She couldn't live forever,' someone said, and that was true. He knew all that. But still, it was robbery, so it was, and in daylight too.

How many years ago was that?

Ah God. He's thinking now of his good friend Wes, bulk-solid as Slieve League, ringing the house, getting through to him on the crackly land line.

'Hold on,' Wes said. 'I'm coming round. I'm on my way. I'll not be long. You'll be okay big man. No, no, just let it out.'

No Sure Acre

What if the North blasts snatch dry at the stone walls

stripping the lichen

bleaching bare the ribs of the man

with no sure acre?

What if hunger scourges his skin

and leaches his land

when there's no gentle ingle nook

to hide him and the spectres come

no hook on which to hang his work a day clothes

in the gloaming?

Where does he go for comfort then in the long pitch-black

when his chair scringes sharp

on the quarry tiles

and dust singes acrid on the grey coiled elements

of his electric bar heater

when he yanks the worn knob of his larder door

to find a single egg

and a tin of Del Monte peaches two years out of date

when his calendar yellows and the pulse of the

Woolworth's clock rattles off beat

and time drags ninety minutes slow?

How will he stanch the wind sucking at him through

slaps

making free with his space

sweeping over his chipped linoleum?

What forces made him settle for the hunched-up crackle

of

The Belfast Newsletter

The Irish News

the fizz of a distant radio station

the solitary slip slide of King James' silken pages

night after night

or prayers to St Jude?

Who does he turn to as he quenches the hard glare of a

hundred naked watts

slamming a defensive bolt home

alone at ten, eleven or twelve

scaling the cracked stairs in stocking feet

to the sheet-less cot he shares with shadows?

Tomorrow he will prise more small potatoes from the

earth

hoking them into the future from the tight patch behind

the byre

furtive as ever in the early half-light

alert as a black bird.

But for now

he oxters his bentness into the curvature of the horsehair

where, lost in its depth,

his hacked fingers patrol the ticking

probing the mattress

searching

stretching for his loaded revolver

before he tries for sleep

untouched by the Sacred Heart

or

the embroidered scripture verse above his head

telling him he is worth more than many sparrows?

Sue Steging

"A Bridge is a place to stare
at water which is already elsewhere"
; Another Westminster Bridge - Alice Oswald

Sue Steging counts herself lucky to have been born in in Liverpool and is still an enthusiastic fan of Liverpool FC. She left to study English and American Literature and then found her way to a career in psychotherapy, learning to listen to the most private of narratives. She began writing for herself in 2018 and thinks that writing poetry has a lot in common with the practice of psychotherapy in its patient search for meaning and resonance, with the added joy of simply playing with words.
Her poems have been published in the Bangor Literary Journal, Issue 11, May 2019 and the Community Arts Partnership Anthology, 'Vision', 2020, 'Heartland', 2021 and 'Threshold', 2022. Sue has been long listed twice for the Seamus Heaney Award with her poems *The Goldfinch*, 2021 and a *naming of parts*, 2022.

Her work can be seen on YouTube in readings for the Bangor Literary Journal, Issue 11, May 2019 https://www.youtube.com/watch?v=GpsYnRlAErk and for the Seamus Heaney Award 28th March 2021, https://www.youtube.com/watch?v=IzmXEJmQMCs&t=1182s

Lines in the Garden

the boundary of the garden has been re-drawn
the lawyers' lines bright red and not to be forgotten
borders leap no more across the neighbours' drives and
hedges
the path to the river no longer crosses no-one's land

but the map is not completely neat and tidy
old acquisitions and easements can still be traced
someone had the grace not to imagine the old oak tree
gone
and let it force a kink into that otherwise straight line

yesterday, I dodged a swallow
not to be interrupted as it darted past
tracing new and pacy diagonals in the air
on its way to a nesting place I had not noticed

and last night with windows open to the mild May air
I woke to the scent of wild garlic
twice it happened and it seemed that I was not the only
one stirring
perhaps a badger was passing by and rustling the moon-
bright flowers

today I followed that green line
interrupted by small diggings
indifferent to all the garden's neatly registered sections
it marks a path only our nighttime neighbours need
remember.

reading a river

bring us news
peaty water
of the higher ground
tell us of earth-slips
pictured in sepia foam
tumbling
where the black rocks stand
speak to us of long dry days
your flow still swift but shallow
a sudden reveal of riverbed
sharp stone and gravel-sand
ice-borne rocks   wall your banks
as if by builders laid
tree roots expose their plaits
and twine to save their upright selves
clay banks fall back   old
paths erode
islands forming and reformed
as fishers
millers
farmers
yoke you to their latest trend
lay pebble banks and weirs
screw engines Archimedes-like
to harness power
flow on peaty water
carving out your river
bearing all our stories
to the sea

Uluru

the Great Pebble
stands
solitary

remnant of old seas
in an ocean of
red earth |

they overlaid
its name
in an invader's
game

spiked
its stone
mysteries

chained
its dreams
to easy habits
of summit |

ancestral ties
restore
a name

but the rains have gone
and the winds are high

we are grounded
in real time |

we thought we were conquerors

taming land
once
live with myth

now
colonised
by flame

Bookshelves

Paint covers varnish on pitch pine pews -
these shelves that once braced congregations
while they read. If timbers pass on
memories and messages through air

as roots once shared their goodness
underground they'd tell of hands
that chose and felled them
shaped them then for decks or docks

or made them sleep to carry rails.
What was it to be shipped to the Americas
as masts? And if not straight and true
then pulped for paper made

into the books that they now hold
with leaves that yellow into brown.
They might be lifted - left behind -
bequeathed - remembered or

remaindered - re-cycled even burned.
Careful names and scribbled notes
mean little now - like palimpsests they
carry hidden histories

we will not bear to know - trace
archetypes and myths that justify
new vengeance - register the rolling tide
of names designed to drown old festivals

with armoured waves - assert the rights
of gods in new disguise to ravage
and reclaim. Perhaps they'd rather be
in that last place and offer their hard comfort

to the few - listen to the creak
of ageing joints - vibrate with fidgets
of the young and facing even there
the fire that's waiting at the end of times to come.

If they are tired now I'll tell them Keats is here -
a sylvan history on a Grecian Urn translates
the words of Aristotle - Augustine - to his
then present tense - points forward

to red poppy fields in unpredicted days -
combines the hopes of youth with cold eternity.
The leaves of beauty truth and goodness
flutter on the branches of these shelves.

The Goldfinch

Rising and falling, wild charms feast happily,
harvesting in the hidden scrub behind farm gates,
perching on spiky seed heads. Small beauties
tease us into envy and the wish to bind.

Charmed, we fancied auguries of health in gold
wing bars, grew fertile in that red-flashed gaze.
Their capture fed our greed for song and beauty,
our wish to see beyond our days.

Witnessing our sickbeds, charmed to divine
our ends; tangled in our allegories, then held
in spells of suffering and salvation, in icons,
and the infant's chubby hands.

Chained to entertain, tricked out to carry water,
Fabritius dulled the charm of stolen song,
dimmed their scarlet cheek guards and claimed
for them the rights of internees.

Though some still mimic song to lure you
in quick-limed limbs of innocent trees, I'm caught up
in charming you with sunny southern seeds. I watch
and see a stoic bird watch me with careful eye.

We failed to foil your charm for camouflage in rough
untended copses, unfarmed fields; for striking out from
ivy laden branches. You flash your yellow epaulettes,
flaunt faces like the bright red coats of grenadiers.

Rhona Stephens

Rhona Stephens was born and raised in Northern Ireland. Having lived at various times in each of the four nations of the United Kingdom, she currently divides her time between Royal Deeside and the Causeway Coast. Books have been her treasured companions on life's pilgrimage. Joining North Coast Writers Group in September 2020, she has found fellow travellers who share her delight in unveiling the power, potential and pleasures of the written word.

Dendrocopos Major

He hangs back,
Bigger but not bolder **than the**

scatter of brash blue tits

u n se t *t* l e d
by five feisty finches
~ charm by name, not by nature ~

Scarce blinking, breathless, I watch, he waits...

                              ...Swift, silent
                                    snatch

... he is gone!

          arcing   way
                his

                  toward   woodland
                  the shadowed

                        to shelter from   and predators
                              prying eyes

Gleanings

A morning chill stilled the air, but the care with which Ruth threw the wrap over her head and drew it close to her body spoke of more than concern for warmth. She glanced right and left before stepping onto the dew-dampened path, heading toward the edge of the village.

The day scarce begun, there was still a dawn hush. Few had stirred, though a woman drawing water from the well acknowledged her as she hurried past. The fragrance of flatbread carried on a breath of wind, reminding Ruth of the gnawing hunger which necessitated this morning's venture. She pressed on, leaving the village behind, rehearsing to herself directions to the field so as not to lose her way.

Two shadows slipped from behind an old cypress tree. Her pace slowed. She moved to the sheltered side of the path, watching the shadows approach the road. Relief replaced anxiety as the forms of Sara and Mariam took shape. She hastened to catch up with them. Safety in numbers.

Exchanging greetings, they set off together for the harvest fields, hoping an early arrival would bring a favourable response to their request for permission to glean. Glean what they could for as long as there was grain to gather - or as long as the owner's grace would allow.

****

The women paused by the side of the road, watching the warp and weft of the barley as the wind stirred the field first one way, then the other. The season was a good one, the grain plump, ripe, plentiful even at the edges where the soil was thinner. Ruth scanned the horizon, noticing a tongue of cloud at rest on a distant hill, hoping, praying it would not rise to trail rain in its wake. The hollow pit in her stomach added urgency to her prayers.

The men were already there, checking the wagon, preparing tools, looking, laughing, nudging, whispering as they stole glances in the direction of the three women. Ruth hesitated, reluctant to step away from her companions or discard her wrap, even though the dew had fled and the sun was already drawing beads of perspiration to her upper lip. But she had to speak to someone.

A quartet of crows dove into the barley. Alerted by a call from a man on the wagon, a lad sprinted towards them, circling his arms, shouting, taking aim with a catapult as the birds made an untidy escape into an olive grove. Laughter from the men brought sharp comment from the man on the wagon. Silence fell as everyone returned to their tasks.

Skirting the edge of the field, Ruth held her wrap secure and made her way to the wagon. The man jumped down as she approached, nodding a greeting. Introducing herself, she dared to look at him before making her request. He was about her age, she reckoned, with a steady gaze which spoke more of respect than boldness. Her apprehension subsided.

"If it please you, sir, I have come to ask if I might glean and gather among the sheaves after your reapers today? I have come early, hoping I might find favour with you, since you are a relative of my father-in-law." She lowered her eyes, balling her fists tight, awaiting his response.

"I am not your relative." The man spoke firmly, but not unkindly. "The owner won't be here till later. But he is a generous man. I have no doubt that he would willingly grant your request. I will speak to him when he comes. Until then, you are welcome to gather what you can. Your friends, too," he added, with a gesture toward Sara and Mariam.

Ruth's thanks came on a breath of appreciation.

****

The women laboured side by side, intermingling with other gleaners, their meagre harvest rising in tandem with the rising sun. It was hard work. It was hot work. It was dusty, dirty, deliberate work. They persevered, pursued by flies, irritated by beetles and bugs, shadowing the men, their gleaning a counterpoint to the regular rhythm of the harvesters' cut.

By the time the foreman called a break, Ruth was trembling with exhaustion, limbs stiff, fingers fumbling to grasp the water bottle she raised to her lips. Cupping a handful of water, she pressed it to her aching neck, welcoming the momentary chill as it mingled with sweat trickling down her back. Weariness threatened to drag her to the ground, a sapping weariness that dulled mind as well as body…and those pangs in her stomach had become a persistent pain. Ruth pushed aside the haunting concern that she might not manage a full day's harvest. She would, she assured herself, she would, she determined, be revived by the break.

A stranger made his way across the field. His bearing, his dress suggested privilege and wealth; the welcome he received from the men revealed warmth and esteem. He spent some time with them before stepping aside to speak privately to the foreman. Both turned toward Ruth, the foreman nodding in her direction. She turned away, a creeping anxiety unsettling her.

****

"My foreman tells me you've been working hard," he called, as he drew near.

She faced him, acknowledging the comment with a nod.

"Yes, sir. We have all laboured hard this morning."

"And you are welcome to stay as long as you wish. Keep close to the other women and when you are thirsty, help yourself to a drink."

"Thank you!" Ruth could not keep the relief from her face or her voice.

The man searched her face. It was not an uncomfortable gaze, more fatherly concern than intrusive stare. She saw him glance at the empty bag by her feet.

"Come now, sit with us awhile."

He pointed toward the men and women shaded beneath a cluster of olive trees.

Ruth hesitated.

"Come, come share bread with us. There's plenty to spare."

He offered with a gentleness that was almost her undoing.

****

Stomach full, thirst quenched, body cool from the shade, Ruth felt almost as refreshed by the kindness she had received as the bread she had eaten. Taking her place behind the reapers again, she glanced across at Sara and Mariam.

Three widows.

Three baskets.

Three families depending on the fragments they would bring home.

No-one would go hungry tonight.

Daily Bread

The smile on my face as I waved them off did not reflect my mood. Or perhaps it did. They will be fed. For the next eight hours my kids will not go hungry. That's enough to force a smile. Breakfast Club, milk, a cooked lunch - I told them to make sure to choose the meal option, not a snack, at lunchtime. And I know, though pretend not to know, that Hazel, the pastoral support teacher, always makes sure they have something for snack time. I owe her. I owe the school. Big time.

But in eight hours the kids will be home. And this evening? Two tablespoons of rice and a small tin of prunes. That...is...it. All that's left from the Foodbank. My purse? I double-checked. Seventeen pence. And I searched pockets and piggybanks, coat linings and cupboards. How has it come to *this*? That I can't provide a meal tonight for my own children. A cup of warm tea, perhaps, though the twins hate tea. And there's no milk. When I think of the days, the years when I threw away leftovers. What I would give now for a couple of crusts or a bowl of Bolognese in the fridge...half a bowl. *How* has it come to this, that so much could be lost, so quickly.

There goes my stomach rumbling, grumbling again. What I would give now for a slice of toast! I'll measure out a cup of water, warm it through and sip it slowly. I know exactly how it has come to this. Tragedy. And treachery. That's how.

Up on that corner shelf is the framed photo of Ben and me on our wedding day. Four years, three girls, two cars, one house. That's the luxury and the limit of all we had together. We would have had another baby. Ben - no, not just Ben. Me too. We both wanted to try again. We would have loved a boy, but we wouldn't have minded. I was just a bit concerned we might have twins again. I wasn't sure how I'd manage that. It was different having twins first time round. But if there are already three to look after…

We were talking about it that morning, that last morning before he left for work. He burnt the toast that day. *It was an accident*, he laughed. And I told him to keep out of the kitchen or he'd stink of burnt toast all day in the office. The smell was still lingering when the police came in. I apologised about it to the policewoman. Apologised! She came to tell me my husband was dead and I apologised for the smell of burnt toast… Ben's death was an accident, too.

That was the tragedy. The treachery was more subtle, but no less brutal. The treachery has brought me to this, has stripped me of everything Ben had been so careful to put in place. *Just in case*, he said. Because Ben *was* careful. He knew the risk of going into partnership with Simon.

And he took advice, because we threw everything into the business. In the end, it came down to who could afford the more expensive lawyer. I don't know how Simon can sleep in his bed at night, knowing what he has done to us...

When I lost the house, we had to move away to find a rental I could afford. I could have got a cheaper place, but I wanted to be in the catchment area of a good school. Ben would have wanted that for the kids. The rental eats up a huge chunk of income, but at least I don't need a car. I need a job, though. You hear about all these unfilled job vacancies, but when you start searching, you find local reality doesn't reflect national publicity. I can't even get a job in the local supermarket. As to getting a teaching post around here... Nothing.

****

I hope the kids had a good lunch, because I still haven't come up with a palatable recipe for prunes and two tablespoons of brown rice. I had another cup of water before I came out to pick them up from school and I did put sugar in this time, so I wouldn't feel faint. That's what happened a few weeks ago. Embarrassing. One of the other mums asked if I was pregnant.

I'm a bit early because I called in to the supermarket on the way, but they haven't reduced the bread yet. We'll check again on our way home.

I can see Hazel, speaking to a man at reception. I wonder what she gave the girls at snack time today…

That man is heading down the corridor. Now Hazel is pressing the button to open the entrance door.

"Emma. Emma, could I have a word, please?"

She beckons me in to her office and clears a seat for me. I hope the girls are ok. And I hope she's not going to ask me for money for anything.

But no, she asks how I am and I ask how she is and… *It's stuffy in here… There's so much glass. The sun overheats this room… My mouth is very dry… I shouldn't have worn this jumper. It's stifling me… I can't breathe!*

"Emma? Emma! Put your head down. Come on. Between your knees… Slowly. Slowly now… Breathe…"

She brings a glass of water and holds it as I sip.

"How often are you getting these attacks?" she asks.

"It's nothing," I mumble. "I… I skipped lunch."

I feel her eyes on me, but don't look up. There's a long silence as I sip the water.

She opens a window, pulls down a blind, draws her chair close, sits down again.

"When did you last eat, Emma?"

Now our eyes do meet.

She spins in her seat, lifts a bag off the back of her chair and rummages.

"Eat this. Now."

She hands me an energy bar.

"And these."

A pack of dried fruit and seeds lands in my lap.

She is still rummaging as I unwrap the bar.

"Only three, I'm afraid. Sorry it's not four." She drops three packs of instant soup into my bag…

"Talk to me, Emma."

But I can't. How pathetic does it sound to tell someone you have nothing. I never asked for anything. Not until I had to. Even now, I tell myself I'm only taking back in benefits what I paid in national insurance. As soon as I get a job, as soon as I can earn enough to make ends meet, I won't have to take another penny.

"It's… it's just a cash flow problem. Things'll be fine."

I've never met anyone with such a steady gaze. She won't stop looking at me. And it's as if in the looking, there is a melting. I feel the fragile mask behind which I hide every time I step outside the front door, I feel it begin to slip.

"I can't find a job," I say, swallowing the tightness in my throat. "I've tried. I mean, I'm still trying. Every day. I can't get anything. I don't mean, I mean… It's not just that I can't get a teaching post. I can't get *anything!* … Well, they did offer to train me as a lorry driver."

"A lorry driver?!"

It's the expression on Hazel's face that does it. I feel laughter erupt from deep in my stomach. Suddenly, we are both laughing, laughing so much that tears trickle down our faces. And it would be fine. Everything would be fine, if only I didn't find - just as suddenly - that my tears are no longer tears of laughter...

Hazel hands me another tissue. I press it to my eyes, waiting for the sobs to subside.

"You've sorted out benefits?"

I nod.

"Sure you've claimed everything you can? For the girls, too?"

I nod again.

"And the Foodbank?"

"Yes."

"Have you heard of Double Day?"

This time, I shake my head.

"Every Friday, 10-12. Pay £5, get double that in goods. I know it's not free, but it would make your money go further. And it's healthy stuff, Emma, not just fillers and fancies. It's organised by the church I go to, the one on the corner at the far end of this road. Local shops and businesses support it. And church members have been bringing surplus from their allotments, too. We had lovely carrots last Friday. Oh! That reminds me…"

Hazel spins her chair again, goes off to a cupboard behind her desk.

"Do you like tomatoes, you and the girls?"

"Love them."

"Good. I've been trying to get rid of these all day. From my greenhouse," she explains, laying a carrier bag half full of plum tomatoes carefully beside me.

"That's really kind of you. Thank you."

"You'll be doing me a favour. I'd hate to throw them out. Almost as much as I'd hate the effort of having to make them into sauce or chutney," she laughs. "I have a glut of courgettes and green beans, too. And potatoes, if you'd like them.'

"Well, if they really are spare and you don't mind. That would be…very kind."

"I'll bring some to school tomorrow. And there'll be more after that if you want them. Everything's done so well at the allotment this year… Now, about Double Day. I'll be there this Friday from 10-11. Then I have to come in to school. What do you think?"

I think of the seventeen pence in my purse. "I don't know… I haven't been to church in a long time." I smile, try to make a joke. "I'm not much of a theologian!"

"You don't have to be a church member or go to church. It's just our way of caring and sharing in the community, Emma. As to not being a theologian… "

Hazel leans back in her chair.

"Don't we all wonder about life at times? About the existence - or not - of God, whether there's purpose to all we go through? We may come up with different answers, but I think we all ask the same big questions." She smiles. "On that basis, there's something of a theologian in each one of us."

"Perhaps."

"Why not give Double Day a try. You don't have to buy anything and there's always free coffee and cake."

"Maybe next week," I say.

****

The girls head for the 'Free Fruit for Kids' stand in the supermarket. I go to the bread section. A staff member is slapping yellow reduction stickers onto a pile of brioches and baguettes. I know they won't, I know they can't possibly be reduced to seventeen pence. But I ask. Sixty-five pence for the brioches, forty for the baguettes.

"Anything else reduced?'

The assistant upends a stack of baguettes, wrinkling her nose as she shakes her head.

"Just this."

She pulls a battered loaf from the bottom of the pile, scans and slaps the sticker on.

146

"Fifteen pence."

I think I misheard. "Fifty?"

"Naw… It's bashed at the corner. Fifteen."

I cradle it in my hands as I head for the checkout.

****

We're having tomato sandwiches for tea. I started making a roly-poly one for myself out of the bashed-at-the-corner bit of the loaf. And guess what. The girls want it. So, I'm trying to slice it like a Swiss roll and they're going to share.

"My turn to say grace," the little one calls.

They always say grace before school dinners. Now the girls won't let us start a meal at home without saying it. They shut their eyes, press palms together and she sing-songs her way through.

"God is great, God is good,
Let us thank him for our food;
By His blessings we are fed
Thank you, Lord, for daily bread."

"A-*men*", they chorus.

"Amen," I whisper.

And I mean it.

Mary Farrell

Mary Farrell, on returning from S.W. France to live in Northern Ireland, joined her first Creative Writing Group in 2017. For the last three years, the Facilitator of the North Coast Writers Group which she co-founded with Robin Holmes, she regularly acts as an Auditor at Creative Writing Workshops at Ulster University and is a member of the Reedsy Online Publishing Company Judging Panel for their weekly Prompts Competitions. Her debut Collection of varied pieces, *'It's like Walking a Tightrope'* was published in 2021, and her second similar collection *'Out of the Chrysalis'* will be published in July 2022. A Collection of her short stories, *'The Kingdom'* will be published in October 2022. She read her story *A Matter of Time* on BBC Radio Ulster, in September 2018, *An autobiographical Tale* on stage at an Tenx9 event, October 2019 and also in 2019 performed at two Open Mic Sessions in Portstewart, Northern Ireland. Her short story, *A Tale of a Barn* won the Lurig Drama Club Competition in 2020, and, recorded by the actor Ciaran Hinds on November 26th, 2020, can be found at www.thenineglens.com. She has had various pieces of Prose and Poetry published in Magazines and Anthologies, both locally in Northern Ireland and internationally.

13 Down

~ an Acrostic of snap- chats ~

Can you promise me? No more secret meetings in this
    cheap motel?

Over my dead body, no more drink for you tonight!

May I be dismissed, Sergeant Major? I've a lot of cleaning
    up to do.

Mummy will kiss it. There… all better now!

Understand darling please, she meant nothing, not like
    you!

No, the Bank won't lend you any more money. You're
    over-stretched as it is.

In Nomine Patri et…..too late, he's gone, Rest in Peace
    my good man.

Could those flaming seagulls keep it down! My
    hangover's killing me!

And did you see her last post on Instagram?

Trust me, you'd never regret sneaking out past your
    parents to meet *me*?

In the goal, you eejit! Not over it!

Oh my beautiful baby boy, how worth the wait you've
    been!

Never… ever… again!

And the Joke's on....

Wedding Announcement from 𝕿𝖍𝖊 𝕻𝖆𝖘𝖆𝖉𝖊𝖓𝖆 𝕾𝖙𝖆𝖗, April 1ˢᵗ, 2019

Congratulations to Marie-Louise Hodgkin, (29) and Seymour Starling 4ᵗʰ, (91) on their marriage today at 12 noon at Pasadena Registry Office, 1570 E. Colorado Blvd, Pasadena. Marie-Louise has been nursing Seymour for three years. When asked by our reporter, Seymour said "I've never felt better". We wish them both a long and happy married life.

~~~

Last Will and Testament of Seymour Starling 4ᵗʰ, lodged & witnessed with Lagerlof, LLP, Pasadena's largest Law Firm, 15.00pm, April 1ˢᵗ , 2019.

'I, Seymour Starling 4ᵗʰ , being of sound mind and body, do hereby leave all of any estates and monies to Marie-Louise Starling. Any re-distribution of the above, I leave to her discretion.

To my three sons and two daughters from my previous marriages, I leave 50$ each. I would like to think they would spend it on a McDonalds Happy Family Meal, celebrating my life.'

~~~

Official Files of Dr. Hoffman, Senior Medical Consultant, Las Encinas Mental Health Hospital, Pasadena, California, April 1st, 2019.

In the presence of the Chief Operating Officer, Corey Castillo from Lagerlof, LLP, I gave Seymour Starling a thorough physical and mental examination at 8.00 am this morning, and I do officially state that he is of sound mind. I concur that he is on strong medication for the physical pain for his Arthritis which confines him to a wheelchair but confirm that this medication has no effect on his mental capacity whatsoever. I wish to go on record as saying:- "In my personal opinion, having known this man since our College years together, he is saner and more settled in his mind than he has been for many years".

~~~

April 2nd, 2019 - Recorded Telephone Conversation, stored in the Thornton Company Safe

(From a Surveillance Report on all telephones in the Starling

*family beach house, authorised by Seymour Starling, 4th,
beginning on March 10th ,2019 to continue throughout April,
carried out by Thornton Investigation Services, Pasadena)*

Male Voice:- Sis, have you seen the paper this morning?
The old bastard's only gone and married her! It's like
some obscene April Fool joke! I'm going straight down to
Lagerlof this morning to check how this affects his will.

Female Voice:- Well, he did hint at it to me. I gave him all
my support of course and promised him I wouldn't tell
the rest of you. As you well know, the Sports business
Grayson and I started would be in serious trouble
without Dad's financial backing to keep it afloat. I need to
keep in with the ole boy!

Male Voice:- You bitch! We might have been able to stop
it! You sold out the rest of us!

Female Voice:- You'd have done the exact same thing to
us …and you know it!

(Sound of phone being slammed down)

~~~

Obituary Notice from **The Pasadena Star**, *October 21st, 2021*

Seymour Starling 4th, 5/7/29 - 20/10/2021 A lifelong resident of Pasadena, Seymour, 93, passed away peacefully at home on October 20th, 2021. After completing the Pasadena school system, Seymour graduated from Harvard Business School, where he was a member of Phi Beta Kappa, and completed a two-year MBA program. He then joined his father's Engineering Company, Seymour Tech. Married three times, Seymour is survived by his third wife Marie-Louise, and their six-month-old son, Seymour Starling 6th. Other survivors include three sons, Seymour Starling 5th, Howard and Stefan, and two daughters, Catherine and Liezl. Seymour was a devoted USC football fan and loved sailing. A memorial service will be held on Saturday, November 6th, 2021, at 12 PM at First Nazarene Church in Pasadena, California.

~~~

All Hallows Eve

shadow fingers creep
  shades cascade from
    a scudding moon
     to blur
      obscure

shapes shimmer into horror
  the night terrorises as
    known becomes unknown
     bewildering
      flickering

light loss
  night gloss
    over a land alien now
     dark with unholy dreams

things go bump
  wings thump
    with irregular beat
     echoing an unsteady heart

time is ajar
  with an hour

        lost

Winter Tree

```
jab
    finger                                              a
         of        t w   i  g          rook-rest
    lightning              c            branch of
        stripped           i            parliament
            b o            c            crowing
              u g          l
arrow  s t r a i g h t     h     e      wind-whipped
    benched                      witch-hair
  girder seat                      decaying
  evening clad              ne…
      with roosting         …st        arthritic
        starling                       limb-bent
          chatter                      gnarled
            leaf naked    strip stripped    spur
                          wood

                    shawl-drape
                    lichen

                    dewdrops
                    dripping

                    spider trails
                  greenwood faces
          roots gouging into bare brown earth
decay   i                                    leaves
berries     n                        desiccated leaves
berries       g                            leaves
```

Up that hill

Jill dragged herself after him. Sweating, panting, she wondered how close she might be to a heart attack.

Come on, you stupid woman, speed it up, we haven't got all day!

It's a steep hill. I'm finding it hard going. Wait a second…just to get my breath!

Nonsense, you're slacking as usual. If you lost some of that fat, it'd be easier. Look at the shape of you. No wonder you're struggling with this little slope.

His voice faded to a steady drone, layered under the loud thrum-beat of her heart. There was no need for them to be climbing anywhere. Situated at the top of the hill, Section A of the Thorpesdale Caravan Site had much prettier views, as well as all its major amenities…*and* it also had vacancies. But no! arriving late last night after dusk, Jack had insisted on a spot in Section C, at the bottom of the hill beside the river.

They say the dawn mists swirling round the viaduct are not to be missed, 8 stars out of 10.

Needless to say, he'd snored his way through the early alarm as she'd lain awake for yet another night, eyes scratching in dry sockets, body screaming for quiet sleep. At home, they'd had separate rooms for years, but there was no escaping each other in the Sprite Super touring caravan he'd rented for the week from his Line Manager at work. *'Promotion through pleasing'* was a mantra of his. She'd suggested going for a week all-inclusive in

Portugal. It took about ten days before he wound down about the horrors of foreign travel, the hazards of foreign food, and above all, about the inferiorities of foreigners themselves. He ceased his tirade only to plan 'The Great Yorkshire Road Trip', sculpting it layer by layer from the pile of Touring Guides he'd borrowed from the Local Library.

So here they were, after a late breakfast fry she'd somehow managed to pull together on the tiny gas stove, carrying empty shopping bags up the steep slope to the Site Supermarket at the top to buy bottled water. It was the only thing they'd run out of among the mountain of provisions he'd listed so carefully and bought so economically the previous week. The daily menus planned assiduously, he couldn't have predicted the depletion of their stockpile of bottled water caused by the unusually warm October weather .

Must be bottled, can't trust tap water. You never know what they're putting in it!

The unexpected disaster began when they were only a few feet from the top of the cobbled path. His Birkenstock sandals, designed to hold their own against the toughest mountain scree, could not withstand exposure to an abandoned, melting ice cream cone. Not foreseeing his downfall -he was looking sideways with lust at a Sprite Super Major 4 (with extra width and four berths) parked just above him. He slipped. Down the slope he plunged, trying to find purchase with his raspberry-rippled soled feet. The more he flailed his arms, the more his speed increased until......

…nearly at the bottom, his head slammed against a small boulder with 'To Section C -Riverside' written on it in red paint. She would have been horrified at the noise of his skull cracking against the rock, but he'd grabbed at her as he'd passed. She'd slipped too and came tumbling after. Thankfully stopping after only a few feet, she sat up and in a befuddled daze, looked down at his body some twenty feet below. His neck and one of his legs were at very unnatural angles. He wasn't moving.

Later, after the Ambulance had taken him to the Hospital Mortuary for the necessary protocols, and her few bruises and cuts had been cleaned and soothed, for a very long time she sat on her own in the caravan, reviewing both the events of the day… and her life to date. As she stood up to make herself a cup of tea, filling the kettle from the caravan water-tank, a thought made her smile.

After the Funeral the first thing I'll do with the Insurance money is book an all-inclusive fortnight in Marbella with a luxury king-sized bed…and I'll sleep like a baby!

Footnote:- 'Jack and Jill' is an English nursery rhyme thought to have been first published in London circa 1765.

North Coast Writers

Made in the USA
Las Vegas, NV
03 April 2022

46824867R00095